NAVIGATING MEDICARE
CHANGE IS INEVITABLE

NAVIGATING
MEDICARE

CHANGE IS INEVITABLE

HILLARY BROOME

WordCrafts

Disclosures
and Important Information

McKnight Advisory Group does not provide legal or tax advice and cannot guarantee rates or issuance of any insurance product. Discussions regarding any tax or legal issues do not constitute legal, tax or accounting advice.

∽

All numbers are time sensitive and are subject to change. The author will provide the year for which figures are correct. For updated figures, consult www.McKnightAdvisory.com Medicare page.

ABOUT THE AUTHOR

Hillary Broome hails from New Smyrna Beach, Florida, and was a minister and missionary in Tennessee and Georgia for over 30 years, both full and part-time. After making a career shift, Hillary started his work at McKnight Advisory Group in October of 2013. He completed his State of Tennessee producer licenses in 2012 and began work as the Advisor for McKnight Advisory Group's Insurance segment. Since starting with McKnight, Hillary has also completed his Certificate for Tennessee Long Term Care Insurance and is a 2014 Graduate of the Leadership in Life Institute (LILI) through the professional association, National Association of Insurance and Financial Advisors (NAIFA).

Over the last nine years, Hillary has trained countless hours to become increasingly familiar with what may seem to be the complicated process that is Medicare. It has become his unique value to meet and build relationships with individuals in our senior community, giving them insight and guidance as they age into Medicare. An important aspect of Hillary's work is preparing for the Annual Election Period which runs from October 15 through December 7 each year, during which time he welcomes new and existing clients to review their Medicare options.

In early 2017, Hillary started working on launching his blog, *Mondays with Mr. Medicare*, at which time he takes a commonly-asked question and answers it based on the Centers of Medicare and Medicaid Services (CMS) guidelines and his personal research and experience with the hundreds of individuals he has helped throughout the years. The popularity of the blog has grown, and the requests for more information from the community have led Hillary and the McKnight team to create and publish this book. McKnight's Passion is Creating Winning Relationships for Life ™ and by providing this information, McKnight hopes to create this winning relationship by giving you the tools you need to make the complicated, uncomplicated when it comes to *Navigating Through the Potholes of Medicare*.

Hillary knows this would not be possible without the help of his team—their natural knack for organization and structure allows for a very thorough and efficient Medicare Process. To Lydia Johnson, "I cannot thank you enough for the hours, support, and dedication you provided with your editing skills on this book, for which we are deeply grateful." Next, to Edwin McKnight, "Thank you for believing in me, training me, and giving me the opportunity to be a servant to our clients."

A personal note from the Author: "To those of you reading, I hope you find value in the information I have provided and that your metamorphosis to Medicare is a smooth and pleasant one."

A Word from the Author
Introduction

Heraclitus, a Greek philosopher of Ephesus, says that "all things pass, and nothing stays," and comparing existing things to the flow of a river, he says "you could not step twice into the same river." Dr. Trudy Foster refers to Heraclitus as saying, "change is the only constant in life." Why then are we surprised when change takes place?

The Law of Constant Change is a fundamental law of our life that needs to be both understood and harnessed if we are to have a happy and successful life. The Law states that, "everything in our life is in constant change, constantly in the process of becoming something else. Nothing stays exactly as it is. Nothing. Movement and change constitute the reality of our being." (John Kehoe)

I graduated from college in 1994 and moved to Toccoa, Georgia, where I preached full time. Heart palpitations had become an every day occurrence, but I was able to bring them under control by sitting down and slowing my breathing.

These episodes would only last for a few minutes but would leave me weak. On one visit back to Tennessee, I woke up with my heart pounding. You could see my chest jumping. This time it lasted for seven or eight hours. Later I found out that my pulse rate was 180 beats per minute. I knew that something was wrong but did not understand the sign. When I made it back to Toccoa, I went to the doctor, and she put me in the ICU with a blood pressure of 240/140. She said I was experiencing Atrial Fibrillation. A change was taking place.

In December of 1999 change reared its ugly head again. I suffered a heart attack which was brought on by having six blockages—75 to 100 percent blocked. They did five bypasses at that time. Later I had an additional three heart attacks, nine stents, a cardiac ablation, a pacemaker/defibrillator, and a watchman, all because of the change that was going on in my body.

It was not until 2013 that I fully saw the change that was happening. After doing an echocardiogram, I learned that my ejection fraction had dropped well below normal. I was having heart failure. While preparing for my watchman surgery in 2022, the doctor did another echocardiogram and discovered my ejection fraction had decreased further and I was informed that my life expectancy was less than a year.

God is so good! I was put on the heart transplant list on December the 7th of 2022. My heart was worn out and there was only one thing that could be done. I received a call from the transplant team on the evening of December the 15th saying they had a heart for me. On December the 16th I was given new life with a 22-year-old heart. My brother-in-law said there was a time when I was heartless. A change had to be made to save my life.

Since that night in December, I have made a lot of changes. First, I lost 25 pounds, which I have kept off because I made a change in what I eat. Eating an apple or vegetables was not allowed until they had been properly scrubbed and soaked in water for two minutes. No grapefruit was allowed, and very little citrus fruit could be eaten. Being in the sun without suntan lotion was not permitted. Walking in the sand without close-toed shoes, and walking in the ocean or swimming in a pool was not allowed. I could not cut my grass or even be outside when my grass was being cut. Absolutely no inhaling the smoke from firewood was allowed. That was rough because I have a wood pellet grill.

Ian Skinner said, "some people do not like change—in life or in business. They like to maintain the same routines and know precisely what will be happening." In her novel *Frankenstein*, Mary Shelly wrote, "Nothing is so painful to the human mind as a great and sudden change."

If you are reading this book, it is likely you have experienced your share of change. Stephanie Martel once said, "Change is inevitable, how you deal with it is optional." Change is a part of life. Nothing can be static for too long. Change is an essential part of life, and so, change is inevitable. No one can live a static life as life requires change. Changes can be in relationships, goals, lifestyle, job roles, etc. We must embrace this aspect and go along with the ups and downs of life. Instead of losing our hearts, we should learn from the issues in our lives.

According to *Definitions from Oxford Languages*, the word

"change" means "to make or become different." It implies making either an essential difference often amounting to a loss of original identity or substitution of one thing for another. A landmark decision leading to change that one makes is at the time one is contemplating Medicare.

Would it not be wonderful if change happened in an instant? Would it not be great to wake up in the morning and think: "I want to start eating better." And then do so? Or decide, "I am going to stop smoking" and never pick up another cigarette? But we all know that is not how change works. It is not a one-time event or singular action—instead, it is a process. And the more we understand the process of change, the more we can empathize, support, and demonstrate compassion for ourselves and those around us who seek to alter their behavior.

What is the process of change? Change is a process involving five stages: pre-contemplation, contemplation, preparation, action, and maintenance. The needs of an individual in one stage of change are different from the needs of an individual in another stage. (The University of Rhode Island: Cancer Prevention Research Center)

DEDICATION

I never met Maiya and did not know that she existed, but she altered my life for good. Who would have thought that a young lady, 22 years old, would impact my life so much. She truly gave me a new opportunity in life. Maiya changed my life. She gave me her heart. I dedicate this book to this young lady who gave so much to a total stranger. I will eat right and do my exercises to protect the gift she shared with me.

Stage One

Pre-contemplation of Medicare

Six Months Out

Introduction

Lack of awareness of a problem is the characteristic of this first stage. Many people do not know that a change to Medicare is up for discussion. As you prepare for your change to Medicare, there are things you will need to know and understand. It is very common to start hearing everyone talking about the plan they selected. All too often, they have Parts and Plans mixed up. Some will be telling you about their Part G when there is no such thing. They speak of medical coverage as Part A instead of Part B. Oh, yes, you will hear people talk about their Advantage plan and call it a supplement plan. My purpose in sharing this is to demonstrate how confusing Medicare can be. I strongly encourage you to learn all about the four Parts of Medicare. You may do this by reading material such as *Medicare and You 2023* or exploring web sites such as Medicare.gov. Another excellent source to learn about Medicare is your local insurance agent. I spend a good part of my time sharing what I have learned with new Medicare clients. As you contemplate the need for a change to Medicare, I would like for you to understand that I do not know all there is to know about Medicare, but every question you ask helps me to evolve into an agent that can help you with your change.

What is Original Medicare?

Original Medicare is one of your health coverage choices which is managed by the federal government. It is comprised of Part A (Hospital) and/or Part B (Medical). As you near your 65th birthday, sometime within the three months before your birth month, you should receive your Medicare Card in the mail if you are drawing Social Security. Sometimes you might hear this card referred to as your "Red, White, and Blue Card." In the event you are not drawing Social Security, you will have to sign up for this card online or through your local Social Security Office.

Finding a doctor that your medical plan accepts can be a nightmare. With Original Medicare you can go to any doctor, other health care provider, hospital, or other facility that is enrolled in Medicare and currently accepts Medicare patients. You can go anywhere in the United States, and if the health care provider is enrolled in Medicare and is accepting new patients you can see them. Note that, generally, Original Medicare does not cover care outside the United States. When selecting a specialist, referrals are not required in most cases. Do not worry about filing those Medicare claims—the law requires providers and suppliers (such as doctors, hospitals, skilled nursing facilities, and home health agencies) to file your claims for the covered services and supplies you get.

The greatest concern you should have with Original Medicare has to do with cost. There is no limit on how much you pay out-of-pocket per year. You generally pay a set amount for your health care (deductible) before Medicare pays its share. Then, Medicare pays its share, and you pay your share (coinsurance /copayment) for covered services and supplies. A monthly premium for Part B should also be expected.

When am I entitled to Original Medicare?

The bill that led to Medicare and Medicaid was signed into law by President Lyndon B. Johnson on July 30, 1965. The original Medicare program included Part A (Hospital Insurance) and Part B (Medical Insurance). Today these two parts are called "Original Medicare." Over the years, Congress has made various changes to the Medicare program. Additional benefits, such as prescription drug coverage, have been offered in more recent years.

Though Medicare and Medicaid started as basic insurance programs for Americans who did not have health insurance, they have changed over the years to provide more and more Americans with access to the quality and affordable health care they need. As time passed, the criteria for Medicare eligibility expanded; and therefore, more individuals became eligible for Medicare coverage.

Medicare is a health benefits program for United States citizens or permanent residents who meet certain work history requirements. In 1972, Medicare was expanded to cover the disabled or certain disability benefits from the Railroad Retirement Board for 24 months, people with end-stage renal disease (ESRD) requiring dialysis or kidney transplant, and people 65 or older that select Medicare coverage. Individuals with Amyotrophic Lateral Sclerosis (ALS—often referred to as Lou Gehrig's disease) were also considered eligible.

Most individuals receive Part A coverage without having to pay a Part A premium. This is because the individual or a spouse paid Medicare taxes while working for a specified duration of time. In 2023, the standard monthly premium for Part B is $164.90 (or higher depending on income).

Individuals with income over $97,000.00, or filing jointly with incomes over $194,000.00, pay a higher premium—up to $560.50 a month in 2023 based on the income related monthly adjustment amount (IRMAA). However, most people who receive Social Security benefits pay less than this amount.

What services does Medicare Part A cover?

In the previous section, I explained that Medicare is one of your health coverage choices which is managed by the federal government and is comprised of Part A (Hospital) and/or Part B (Medical). I will now address the services that Medicare covers under Part A. In short, Medicare covers certain medical services and supplies in hospitals, doctors' offices, and other health care settings. Services are covered either under Part A or under Part B.

Part A (Hospital Insurance) helps cover: Inpatient care in a hospital; Inpatient care in a skilled nursing facility (not custodial or long-term care); Hospice care; Home health care; and Inpatient care in a religious nonmedical health care institution.

In the event you require blood, it may be obtained from a blood bank at no charge. You will not have to pay for it or replace it. If the hospital must buy blood for you, you must either pay the hospital costs for the first three units of blood you receive in a calendar year, donate the blood yourself, or have someone else donate for you.

To qualify for hospice care, a hospice doctor and your doctor (if you have one) must certify that you are terminally ill, meaning you have a life expectancy of six months or less. If you do qualify, coverage includes:

- All items and services needed for pain relief and symptom management
- Medical, nursing, and social services
- Medications
- Certain durable medical equipment
- Aide and homemaker services
- Other covered services, as well as services Medicare usually does not cover, such as spiritual and grief counseling.

Staying overnight in a hospital does not always mean you are an inpatient. You only become an inpatient when a hospital formally admits you as an inpatient after a doctor orders it. For more information on this issue please refer to Medicare and You 2022, pages 27–29.

What services does Medicare Part B cover?

Medicare Part B (Medical Insurance) helps cover medically necessary doctors' services, outpatient care, home health services, durable medical equipment, mental health services, and other medical services. Part B also covers many preventive services.

Generally, with most covered preventive services, provided by a doctor or other qualified health care provider who accepts assignment, there is no charge. However, for some preventive services, you may have to pay a deductible, coinsurance, or both. These costs may also apply if you get a preventive service in the same visit as a non-preventive service.

Covered preventive services include:

- Abdominal aortic aneurysm screening
- Advance care planning
- Alcohol misuse screening and counseling
- Ambulance services
- Ambulatory surgical centers
- Blood
- Bone mass measurement (bone density)
- Cardiac rehabilitation
- Cardiovascular disease (behavioral therapy)
- Cardiovascular disease screenings
- Cervical and vaginal cancer screenings
- Chemotherapy
- Chiropractic services (limited coverage)
- Chronic care management services
- Clinical research studies
- Colorectal cancer screenings
  One or more of these tests may be covered:
  § Multi-target stool DNA test
  § Screening fecal occult blood test
  § Screening flexible sigmoidoscopy
  § Screening colonoscopy
  § Screening barium enema
- Continuous Positive Airway Pressure (CPAP) therapy
- Defibrillator (implantable automatic)
- Depression screening
- Diabetes screenings
- Diabetes self-management training
- Diabetes supplies
- Doctor and other health care provider services
- Durable medical equipment (DME)

- EKG or ECG (electrocardiogram) screening
- Emergency department services
- Eyeglasses (after cataract surgery)
- Federally Qualified Health Center (FQHC) services
- Flu shots
- Foot exams and treatment
- Glaucoma tests
- Hearing and balance exams
- Hepatitis B shots
- Hepatitis C screening test
- Home health services
- Kidney dialysis services and supplies
- Kidney disease education services
- Laboratory services
- Lung cancer screening
- Medical nutrition therapy services
- Mental health care (outpatient)
- Obesity screening and counseling
- Occupational therapy
- Outpatient hospital services
- Outpatient medical and surgical services and supplies
- Physical therapy
- Pneumococcal shot
- Prescription drugs (limited)
- Prostate cancer screenings
- Prosthetic/orthotic items
- Pulmonary rehabilitation
- Rural Health Clinic (RHC) services
- Second surgical opinions

- Sexually transmitted infection (STI) screening and counseling
- Shots*
  Part B covers:
  § Flu shots
  § Hepatitis B shots
  § Pneumococcal shots

*Note about the shingles shot: The shingles shot is not covered by Part A or Part B. Generally, Medicare prescription drug plans (Part D) cover the shingles shot, as well as all commercially available vaccines needed to prevent illness. Contact your Medicare drug plan for more information about coverage.

- Smoking and tobacco-use cessation (counseling to stop smoking or using tobacco products)
- Speech-language pathology services
- Surgical dressing services
- Telehealth
- Tests (other than lab tests)
- Transitional care management services
- Transplants and immunosuppressive drugs
- Travel (health care needed when traveling outside the United States, see Unit Three for more information)
- Urgently needed care
- "Welcome to Medicare" preventive visit
- Yearly "Wellness" visit

Some of the items and services that Original Medicare does NOT cover include:

✗ Most dental care
✗ Eye examinations related to prescribing glasses
✗ Dentures
✗ Cosmetic surgery
✗ Acupuncture
✗ Hearing aids and exams for fitting hearing aids
✗ Long-term care
✗ Concierge care (also called concierge medicine, retainer-based medicine, boutique medicine, platinum practice, or direct care)

Please consult *Medicare and You 2023* on pages 30–54 for a complete explanation of preventive services.

Are Medicare Advantage plans right for me?

The first advantage-type plan was Medicare + Choice which began in 1997. In 2003, it became the prototype for what we now know as Medicare Advantage. It was not until 2005 that these plans gained an increase in insurer participation. The popularity of these plans has grown from zero in 1997 to over 21 million in 2018 (35% of the people on Medicare are on an Advantage plan). Some are suggesting that from the statistics, it appears as though Medicare Advantage plans are continuing to gain popularity. For this reason, you should consider if a Medicare Advantage plan is a good fit for your medical care.

Private insurance companies approved by Medicare offer Medicare Advantage plans (also known as "Part C" or "MA Plans"). You must be entitled to Medicare Part A and have your Part B to sign up for a Medicare Advantage plan.

Medicare pays a fixed amount for your care each month to the companies offering Medicare Advantage plans. These companies must follow rules set by The Centers of Medicare and Medicaid Services (CMS). The insurance company has agreed with (CMS) to manage the insured's health benefits. These plans must cover all the services provided by Medicare, and in most cases, exceed these services. Insurance companies do this by adding extra coverage, such as vision, hearing, dental, routine transportation to medical appointments, chiropractic services, and fitness plans. Most Advantage plans also include annual physical exams, in-home safety assessments, over-the-counter drugs, and Medicare Part D (prescription drug coverage).

When speaking of Medicare Supplement plans (Medigap plans), I generally refer to them as the "roof on the house"— meaning it helps to keep your expenses from going too high. The "Maximum Out of Pocket" expense (MOOP) is how Medicare Advantage plans do the same. Each plan will include a MOOP expense that states the most coinsurance and copayments you will pay for Part A and Part B services.

Medicare Advantage plans must cover all Part A and Part B benefits. In addition to those benefits, it must also cover cost-sharing benefits equivalent to those covered under Original Medicare. All plans must cover the following services even when provided by non-network providers: emergency services; out-of-area urgently needed services; and out-of-area renal dialysis. (See Charts & Data—Chart # 2)

If I do not take any prescription medications, do I still need a drug card?

Medicare offers prescription drug coverage to everyone with Medicare. Individuals entitled to Part A and/or enrolled under Part B are eligible to enroll in Part D plans. The beneficiary must live in the plan's service area. Coverage under Medicare Part D benefits is provided by private companies.

The official answer to this question is *yes*; however, you can elect not to have a drug card. If you do not take many prescription medications at the current time, you should consider joining a Medicare drug plan. If you decide not to join a Medicare drug plan when you are first eligible, and you do not have other creditable prescription drug coverage, and you do not get Extra Help, you will likely pay **a late enrollment penalty** if you join a plan later. Generally, you will pay this penalty for as long as you have Medicare prescription drug coverage. To get Medicare prescription drug coverage, you must join a plan approved by Medicare that offers Medicare drug coverage.

You should also consider the issue of Enrollment Periods. When you first become eligible for Medicare, you can join during your Initial Enrollment Period. If you get Part B for the first time during the General Enrollment Period, you can also join a Medicare drug plan. Enrollment is between January 1–March 31 each year, and your coverage will start July 1 of that year. This will increase the months you are without Part D coverage, and as a result, will increase your penalty. During Open Enrollment—between October 15– December 7 each year, you may enroll in a Part D Plan. Your coverage will begin on January 1 of the following year. This too could lengthen your months without coverage, thus increasing your penalty.

As to creditable prescription drug coverage, if you have employer or union coverage, call your benefits administrator to verify that their coverage is at least as good as Medicare. Always contact your benefits administrator before you make any changes, or before you sign up for any other coverage. If you drop your employer or union coverage, you may not be able to get it back. You also may not be able to drop your employer or union drug coverage without also dropping your employer or union health (doctor and hospital) coverage. If you drop coverage for yourself, you may also have to drop coverage for your spouse and dependents.

What are Medicare Supplement Insurance (Medigap) policies?

Original Medicare is coverage managed by the federal government. You generally must pay a portion of the cost for each service covered by original Medicare. You will have original Medicare unless you choose a Medicare Advantage plan, such as an HMO or PPO.

Medicare does not cover everything, and even if a service or item is covered, you may be left exposed to high out-of-pocket costs with all the co-payments, coinsurance, and deductibles, which you will have to pay yourself. Original Medicare pays for many, but not all, of the costs for health care services and supplies. Some of the items and services that Medicare does not cover include:

✗ Most dental care
✗ Eye examinations related to prescribing glasses
✗ Dentures

✗ Cosmetic surgery

✗ Acupuncture

✗ Hearing aids and examinations for fitting them

✗ Long-term care

Private insurance companies sell Medicare Supplement Insurance policies to help pay some of the remaining health care costs. These Medicare Supplement Insurance policies are also called Medigap policies. Such policies offer coverage for services that Original Medicare does not cover, such as medical care when you travel outside the United States, as well as some deductibles, coinsurance, and/or co-payments. Medigap policies are not required, but can you imagine building a house and not putting a roof on it? What would be the outcome? Your heat would go up into the clouds. This would be equivalent to your dollar bills flitting up into the sky. Medicare without a supplement plan would do the same. You, the client, would be responsible for paying those high co-payments, coinsurance, and deductibles. The supplement plans will keep your costs from getting out of reach.

"Standardized" policies, identified in most states by letters A through D, F and G, and K through N, have been set up by federal and state laws to protect you. These plans must be clearly acknowledged as "Medicare Supplement Insurance."

As of January 1, 2020, Medigap plans sold to new people with Medicare are not allowed to cover the Part B deductible. Because of this, Plans C and F are not available to people new to Medicare starting on January 1, 2020. If you already have either of these two plans (or the high deductible version of Plan F) or are covered by one of these plans before January 1, 2020, you will be able to keep your plan. If you were eligible for Medicare before January 1, 2020, but not yet enrolled, you may be able to buy one of these plans.

Individuals purchasing a Medigap plan from a private insurance company MUST have Part A and Part B. Only one policy holder is covered with each policy and monthly premiums MUST be made to the private insurance company. The preferred time to enroll in a Medigap plan is during the Open Enrollment Period which begins the first day of the month you turn age 65 and continues for a period of six months. You can delay enrolling in Part B if you have group health coverage provided by your or your spouse's current employer. If you select this option, your Medigap Open Enrollment period will start when you sign up for Part B.

Medigap is NOT a Medicare Advantage health plan or other Medicare health plan and only supplements Original Medicare benefits. A Medigap plan cannot be used with a Medicare Advantage health plan, and it is against the law to sell a Medigap plan to someone already in a Medicare Advantage health plan. Individuals who are enrolled in Medigap plans may only obtain Medicare drug coverage (Part D) through a stand-alone prescription drug plan. (See note on—Chart # 3)

Author's Insights and Conclusion

I strongly suggest that you start your change to Medicare no less than six months prior to your 65th birthday. As you can tell from what you have read so far, Medicare is overwhelming without a doubt. Medicare consists of four Parts: Part A, Part B, Part C, and Part D. We have discussed what each of these covers and does not cover. This information will aid you in the next segment in selecting a product that will support and define your individual medical insurance or coverage needs. (See notes on—Chart # 1)

During this time frame, (you should) select an independent insurance agent who can answer any questions you may have regarding how each of these Parts works to fulfill your needs. You will need to have a conversation with your doctors to verify that they do accept Medicare. This is of the greatest importance because in the event your doctors do not accept Medicare, sometimes it takes months to establish a relationship with a new doctor. I did not address this issue of doctors and Medicare Advantage plans in this unit, but I will go into these matters in Unit Two. As you come into the 90-day window prior to your 65th birthday, there will be a narrowing down of the vision for your Medicare needs.

Stage Two

Contemplation of Medicare

90 Days, 30 Days, And Effective Date

Introduction

During the Contemplation stage, one has become more knowledgeable of Medicare and is now looking at the pros and cons. They are not sure they need to make a change from their group plan to Medicare. It is important to weigh out the benefits of both choices. Would it be in my best interest to stay on my group plan? Do I have to make a change? Can I stay on my spouse's plan?

When you enter the 90-day period just before your 65th birthday, a new set of questions arises. Now it is all about the should I, how much, and the what ifs. There are many road signs directing you along this journey, so keep a sharp eye out and be prepared because timing can make all the difference on your arrival.

How much does Part B coverage cost?

In Unit One I briefly explained what Part B covers. I will now cover the basic cost of Medicare Part B in 2023—who pays less, and who pays more.

It is suggested that 95% of people on Medicare pay the standard Part B premium amount of $164.90 in 2023. If you have a higher income, you will pay an additional premium amount for your Medicare Part B and Medicare Part D. You will pay the standard premium amount (or higher) if:

- You enroll in Part B for the first time in 2023
- You do not get Social Security benefits
- You are directly billed for your Part B premiums (meaning they are not taken out of your Social

Security benefits)

- You have Medicare and Medicaid, and Medicaid pays your premiums (Your state will pay the standard premium amount of $164.90)
- Your modified adjusted gross income as reported on your IRS tax return from two years ago is above a certain amount. If so, you will pay the standard premium amount and an Income Related Monthly Adjustment Amount (IRMAA), which is an extra charge added to your premium (See Charts and Data—Chart #5)

According to Medicare.gov, most beneficiaries pay only 25% of the total premium cost for Part B, leaving the remaining 75% to be paid by the government. Individuals with higher incomes, based on the income reported to the Internal Revenue Service (IRS), pay a larger percentage of the total cost for Part B. A beneficiary will pay monthly Part B premiums equal to 35, 50, 65, or 80 percent of the total cost, depending on what is reported to the IRS.

What if I have a medicine that is "rocking the boat"?

Do you have one medicine that is "rocking the boat" and costs too much? If so, what options do you have?

Coverage of Medicare Part D (Drug Card) benefits is provided by private companies. Medicare pays a share of the program costs. Individuals who are entitled to Part A and/or enrolled under Part B are eligible to enroll in Part D plans. The beneficiary must live in the plan's service area.

For 2023, the standard benefit requires the beneficiary to pay up to a $505.00 deductible, then 25% of prescription drug costs between $505.00 and $4,660.00 = $1,038.75. This is called the initial coverage period. After total spending on drugs (by the beneficiary, by certain subsidy programs, and by the plan) reaches $4,660.00, then the beneficiary moves into the "Coverage Gap," sometimes called the *Donut Hole*. In this stage, the beneficiary pays 25% of generic drug costs and 25% of brand name drug undiscounted costs.

Once the beneficiary's expenditures reach a total of $7,400.00, the beneficiary is through the Coverage Gap and reaches catastrophic coverage. On any future prescriptions, the beneficiary pays either a co-pay of $4.15 for generic drugs and $10.35 for brand name drugs or a co-insurance of 5%, whichever is greater.

It is easy to see that your out-of-pocket costs can quickly become expensive. All it takes is one medicine for your monthly costs to become unbearable. I call these medicines "troublemakers." There are two terms that you need to be aware of when considering a Drug Card. A formulary is simply a list of drugs covered by the plan. To market a Drug Card, the insurance company must include at least two drugs in each therapeutic category. The more they include, the greater the chances your medicine will be on the formulary. If your medicine is not on the formulary, you will pay the full cost. Enrollees have the right to request a formulary exception either for coverage of non-formulary drugs or for coverage of formulary drugs at a less costly formulary tier. The second term is cost-sharing tiers. Drugs may be grouped together by amount of cost-sharing. Many plans group drugs into four of five tiers, with lower tiers costing less than higher tiers.

Your agent will help you find a Drug Card that has all

your medicines on the formulary with as low a tier level as possible. This assists you in keeping drug costs down. You may be asking, but what about that "troublemaker"? Sometimes, step therapy is required by insurance companies. This is where one or more similar lower cost drugs must be tried before other costlier drugs are tried. If a doctor thinks an enrollee needs a drug that is not on the formulary, the enrollee or the doctor may apply for a formulary exception. To facilitate that request, a standard form is available on Part D plan websites for enrollees to request a coverage determination, including a formulary exception. If a beneficiary has limited income and resources, they may qualify for the low-income subsidy (LIS) to cover all or some of the Part D plan premium and cost-sharing.

Part B immunosuppressive drug coverage

Medicare covers kidney transplants for people suffering from end-stage renal disease regardless of age. If you're under 65, however, Medicare only covers vital immunosuppressive drugs for 36 months after the operation.

What does creditable coverage mean?

Often a client will ask if he or she can stay on their current coverage with the company they are working for. When this question is asked, the first issue I will explain is the need for "creditable coverage." This comes into play with prescription drug coverage that is expected to pay, on average, at least as much as Medicare's standard prescription drug coverage (for example, from an employer or union). Individuals who have this kind of coverage (from an employer or union) when they become eligible for Medicare can generally keep that coverage without paying a penalty if they decide to enroll in Medicare prescription drug coverage later.

All beneficiaries who do not maintain creditable coverage must pay a Part D late enrollment penalty if they wish to enroll in Part D. There is **a permanent premium penalty** of one percent of the national standard premium for every month that a beneficiary could have had Part D coverage, or equivalent creditable coverage and chose not to enroll. There is no penalty for individuals who qualify for low-income assistance.

Employers/unions will notify their employees of whether their prescription drug coverage is "creditable" (coverage that, on average, equals at least as much as Medicare's standard Part D coverage expects to pay) via an annual statement. Beneficiaries having creditable drug coverage through Tri-Care, the VA, or the FEHBP could also benefit from the advantage of "creditable coverage." Always compare your plan to coverage with available Part D plans when deciding whether to enroll in Part D.

Should I consider delaying enrollment in Medicare Part A and Part B?

I recommend that you should always contact your employer or union benefits administrator before delaying enrollment in Part A and Part B to verify an explanation as to how your insurance works with Medicare. Your employer coverage may require that you enroll in Part A and Part B to get your full coverage. Before making your decision, you should read the seven scenarios below and select the one that best applies to your situation:

1.   I currently have health insurance from a previous employer (including COBRA or retiree health insurance)

You should enroll in Part A and Part B when you turn age 65. Delaying this could cause a gap in your coverage, and you may have to pay **a lifetime late enrollment penalty**. The longer you wait, the more the increase in the amount of the penalty.

2.   I have TRICARE or CHAMPVA coverage

Your decision to enroll in Part A and Part B depends on whether you are eligible for premium-free Part A:

Definition: Premium-free Part A: Most individuals get Part A coverage without having to pay a Part A premium. This is because they or a spouse paid Medicare taxes while working for a specified duration of time (40 quarters or ten years).

- I am eligible for premium-free Part A: You are required to enroll in both Part A and Part B to keep your TRICARE or CHAMPVA coverage.
- I am NOT eligible for premium-free Part A: Enrolling in Part A and Part B is optional; but if you do not enroll during your Initial Enrollment Period, you will have to wait to sign up, and you may have to pay **a lifetime late enrollment penalty**—and the amount of that penalty increases the longer you wait.

3.   I have health insurance based on my (or my spouse's) current employment, from an employer with 20 or more

employees (this includes those with Federal Employees Health Benefits (FEHB))

NOTE: If you have COBRA or retiree coverage, or if your employer gives you an amount of money to purchase health insurance, you do NOT have health insurance based on "current employment." If you have one of these types of insurance, you should look at the other options in this unit.

Your decision to enroll in Part A and Part B depends on whether you have a high-deductible health plan with a health savings account (HSA):

- I do NOT have a Health Savings Account (HSA)

Part A: If you qualify for premium-free Part A, you should enroll in Part A when you turn age 65. However, if you must pay a premium for Part A, you can delay Part A until you (or your spouse) stop working or lose that employer coverage. You will NOT pay a penalty for delaying Part A if you enroll within eight months of losing your coverage or stopping work (whichever happens first).

Part B: You can delay Part B until you (or your spouse) stop working or lose that employer coverage. This allows you to save the cost of your Part B premium. It also allows you to postpone your one-time "Medigap open enrollment period" until a later time, when you may want to purchase this type of coverage. You will NOT pay a penalty for delaying Medicare if you enroll within eight months of losing your coverage or stopping work, whichever happens first. You will want to plan and enroll in Part B at least a month before you either stop working or your employer coverage ends so you do not have a gap in coverage.

- I have a High-Deductible Health Plan AND a Health Savings Account (HSA)

Once you enroll in any part of Medicare, you will not be able to contribute to your HSA. If you would like to continue making contributions to your HSA, you can delay both Part A and Part B until you (or your spouse) stop working or lose that employer coverage. You will NOT pay a penalty for delaying Medicare if you enroll within eight months of losing your coverage or stopping work, whichever happens first. You should talk with your employer benefits manager about whether it makes sense to delay enrolling in Part A and Part B.

NOTE: If you qualify for premium-free Part A, your coverage will be retroactive up to six months from when you sign up. So, you should stop making contributions to your HSA six months before you enroll in Part A and Part B (or apply for Social Security benefits, if you want to collect retirement benefits before you stop working).

4.   I have health insurance based on my (or my spouse's) current employment from an employer with fewer than 20 employees

NOTE: If you have COBRA or retiree coverage, or if your employer gives you an amount of money to purchase health insurance, you do NOT have health insurance based on "current employment." If you have one of these types of insurance, you should find that scenario in this unit.

You should enroll in Part A and Part B when you turn

age 65. In this case, Medicare pays before your employer insurance. This means that Medicare is the primary payer for your health coverage.

5. I have health insurance from the Health Insurance Marketplace or other private insurance not directly offered by my employer

NOTE: The Individual Health Insurance Marketplace is a place where people can go to compare and enroll in health insurance. In some states, the Marketplace is run by the state; and in other states, it is run by the federal government. The Health Insurance Marketplace was set up through the Affordable Care Act.

If you are eligible for premium-free Part A, you should enroll in Part A and Part B when you turn age 65. If you have Marketplace coverage, and you are getting the reduced premium or tax credit, it will stop once your Medicare Part A starts. You will not need this coverage once Medicare begins.

!WARNING! If you are not eligible for premium-free Part A, you can choose to stay in the Individual Health Insurance Marketplace to get your coverage. That coverage may cost less; but if you choose to enroll in Medicare Part A and/or Part B later, you will have to wait to sign up, and you may have to pay **a lifetime late enrollment penalty**—and the amount of that penalty increases the longer you wait.

6. I have Veterans Affairs (VA) coverage
If you have only Veterans Affairs (VA) coverage, you should

enroll in Part A and Part B when you turn age 65. If you also have coverage described in one of the scenarios above, you should use the information contained in that scenario to decide whether to enroll in Part A and Part B.

! WARNING ! If you do not enroll in Part A and Part B during your Initial Enrollment Period, you will have to wait to sign up, and you may have to pay **a lifetime late enrollment penalty**—and the amount of that penalty increases the longer you wait.

7.   I do NOT have health insurance

You should enroll in Part A and Part B when you turn age 65.

! WARNING ! If you do not enroll in Part A and Part B during your Initial Enrollment Period, you will have to wait to sign up, and you may have to pay **a lifetime late enrollment penalty**—and the amount of that penalty increases the longer you wait.

What if I want to work past the age of 65?

Individuals already receiving benefits from Social Security, or the Railroad Retirement Board (RRB), will automatically get Part A and Part B starting the first day of the month they turn age 65. Individuals not receiving benefits from Social Security or the Railroad Retirement Board (RRB) may sign up for Parts A and B during their initial enrollment period, which begins three months before their 65th birthday, includes the month they turn age 65 and ends three months after their 65th birthday.

You may elect to continue working past age 65, but I suggest that you speak with your Human Resources Department to make sure the group coverage is equivalent "creditable coverage" for Part B and Part D. If the group is greater than 20 employees, the group plan pays primary, and Medicare pays secondary. In this case you can opt out of Part B and have coverage with the group. If the group has fewer than 20 employees, Medicare pays primary, and the group pays secondary. I encourage you to have your HR department check with its Insurance Carrier to see if they will pay without your being enrolled in Part B.

Qualifiers who have group health plan coverage based on their own current employment or the current employment of a spouse may enroll in Part B any time while covered under the group health plan or during a special enrollment period that occurs during the eight-month period immediately following the last month of the group coverage.

For individuals who do not enroll in Part B when first eligible, the Part B premium is increased 10% for each full 12-month period the beneficiary could have had Part B but did not enroll. This is known as a "late enrollment penalty." A form called a "Request for Employee Information" will be needed when you apply for Part B and when applying for Medicare Part D showing there was creditable coverage. This form will help you to avoid any penalties.

There is **a permanent premium penalty** of one percent of the national standard premium for every month that a beneficiary could have had Part D coverage, or equivalent creditable coverage, and chose not to enroll. There is no penalty for individuals who qualify for low-income assistance.

If I am working for an employer with fewer than 20 employees, do I have to have Part B?

Beneficiaries enrolled in Part B must pay a monthly premium. In 2023, the standard monthly premium for Part B is $164.90 (or maybe higher depending upon your income); however, most people who get Social Security benefits pay $164.90. For individuals who do not enroll in Part B when first eligible, the Part B premium is increased 10% for each full 12-month period the beneficiary could have had Part B but did not enroll. This is known as a "late enrollment penalty."

If you or your spouse (or family member if you are disabled) is still working and you have health coverage through that employer or union, contact your employer or union benefits administrator to find out how your coverage works with Medicare. This includes federal or state employment and active-duty military service. It might be to your advantage to delay Part B enrollment. You can sign up for Part B without paying a penalty any time you have health coverage based on your or your spouse's current employment (or a family member's current employment if you are disabled).

When you have other insurance (such as employer group health coverage) and Medicare, there are rules that decide whether Medicare or your other insurance pays first. Use this chart to see who pays first. (See Charts & Data—Chart # 7)

If you or your spouse are working for a group with less than 20 employees, Medicare pays first. For this reason, it is important that you speak with your employer or union benefits administrator to see how your current insurance pays. If you do not have Part B, your insurance carrier may not pay.

My spouse is aging into Medicare, so what do I do?

My spouse is aging into Medicare, but I do not for another three years. He or she currently has group coverage and carries me on his or her employer's plan. When he or she retires this year, what do I do?

This question has many layers, so there is no short answer. Here are some various scenarios to consider:

Scenario #1: If your spouse (the primary insured) ends the group coverage to sign onto Medicare, you (the beneficiary) will have to secure health insurance from another source, such as COBRA (if eligible), an individual policy, or your employer's plan (if you have access to this coverage).

Scenario #2: If your spouse (the primary insured) ends the group coverage to sign onto the retirement medical plan that the group offers, you (the beneficiary) must check with the employer's benefits administrator or the union group benefits administrator to see if you, as the retiree's spouse, can be included on the retiree's medical plan. If the answer is no, you (the beneficiary) will have to secure health insurance from another source, such as COBRA (if eligible), an individual policy, or your employer's plan (if you have access to this coverage). If the answer is yes, you will then need to confirm if you will be required to come off the retirement plan when you turn age 65.

Scenario #3: Your spouse (the primary insured) may elect

to continue working until you (the beneficiary) age into Medicare, and then both of you will sign onto Medicare at the same time.

Please keep in mind, if Scenarios #2 or #3 are elected, your spouse must determine if he or she is required to take Part B. If not, your spouse will need to complete Social Security's "Request for Employment Information" form to prevent paying a Part B late entry penalty when he or she finally terminates the group coverage (Scenario #3).

Author's Insights and Conclusion

If your head is spinning after reading this Unit, do not feel bad because you are now in the majority. This is the time of contemplation, and your selection can impact your finances, your medical care, and your peace of mind. The one thing I would like to impress upon you is that **now is the time to ask for help**. Hopefully by now you have selected an insurance agent who will be able to help you with the timing issues, how to alter your path to avoid the potholes, and how to make decisions on whether to continue working, including the impact that choice will have on your spouse.

STAGE THREE

PREPARATION FOR MEDICARE

Introduction

You are now ready to make a commitment to change. Medicare is clearly in sight, and you intend to move forward. Now that I have made a commitment to change, how do I make this change?

How and when can I sign up for Medicare Part A and Part B?

Medicare is administered by the Centers for Medicare & Medicaid Services (CMS), an agency of the U.S. Department of Health and Human Services. Medicare is a health benefits program for United States citizens or permanent residents who meet certain work history requirements:

- Age 65 or older
- Under age 65 with certain disabilities
- All who get disability benefits from Social Security or certain disability benefits from the Railroad Retirement Board for 24 months
- Individuals with Amyotrophic Lateral Sclerosis (ALS), often referred to as Lou Gehrig's Disease
- Individuals with end-stage renal disease (ESRD)

Signing up for Social Security benefits is not a prerequisite for having Medicare, but it does affect how Medicare is obtained. Your consideration of the issues comes after you have decided whether to enroll in Medicare Part A and Part B when you turn age 65 or whether you should delay enrollment in Medicare Part A and Part B. Some people will be automatically enrolled in Part A and Part B, while others can only get Part A and Part B if they complete an application with Social Security. So, you first need to figure out which applies to you.

I WILL be getting benefits from Social Security (or the Railroad Retirement Board (RRB)) at least four months before I turn age 65:

If you get benefits from Social Security (or the RRB) at least four months before you turn age 65, you do not need to do anything to get Part A and Part B. You will automatically get Part A and Part B starting the first day of the month you turn age 65. (If your birthday is on the first day of the month, Part A and Part B will start the first day of the prior month.)

This is when you should start watching the mail box. A "Welcome to Medicare" package, which will include your Medicare "red, white and blue card," should arrive approximately three months before your 65th birthday. Included in this package will be a brochure about the Medicare program and your options for getting your Medicare coverage. You should contact the Social Security Office if you do not receive your package with your Medicare card within this time frame.

I WILL NOT be getting benefits from Social Security or the Railroad Retirement Board (RRB) at least four months before I turn age 65:

If you are not getting benefits from Social Security (or the RRB) at least four months before you turn age 65, you will need to apply with Social Security to get Part A and Part B. If you want your Part A and Part B coverage to start when you turn age 65, you will need to sign up during the three months before you turn age 65. You may sign up as follows:

- Apply for Social Security online at SocialSecurity.gov, visit your local Social Security Office, or call Social Security at 1-800-772-1213. TTY users should call 1-800-325-0778.
- Call RRB, if you worked for a railroad, at 1-877-772-5772. TTY users should call 1-312-751-4701.

! WARNING ! If you wait until the month you turn age 65 (or the three months after you turn age 65) to enroll, your Part B coverage will be delayed. This could cause a gap in your coverage.

What if you elect to delay Part B, but start Part A when you turn age 65? How is this done?

I WILL be getting benefits from Social Security (or the Railroad Retirement Board (RRB)) at least four months before I turn age 65:

Unless you contact Social Security, you will automatically get BOTH Part A and Part B starting the first day of the month you turn age 65. (If your birthday is on the first day of the month, Part A and Part B will start the first day of the prior month.) **Example:** Birthday 09/01/1958 would give you an effective date for Part A and Part B of 08/01/2023.

If you want to delay your Part B coverage, you must refuse

Part B before your Medicare coverage has begun. You have two options for refusing Part B:

1. Follow the instructions that come with the card and send the card back. If you keep the card, you are keeping Part B and will pay Part B premiums.
2. Contact Social Security at 1-800-772-1213 (TTY 1-800-325-0778).

I WILL NOT be getting benefits from Social Security or the Railroad Retirement Board (RRB) at least four months before I turn age 65:

If you are not getting benefits from Social Security (or the RRB) at least four months before you turn age 65, you will need to apply with Social Security to get Part A. You will sign up as follows:

-   Apply for Social Security online at SocialSecurity.gov, visit your local Social Security Office, or call Social Security at 1-800-772-1213. TTY users should call 1-800-325-0778.
-   Call RRB, if you worked for a railroad, at 1-877-772-5772. TTY users should call 1-312-751-4701.

The decision to delay your Part B should only be considered in light of whether you or your spouse are still working and have coverage through the group plan for that employer. You should start your Part B coverage as soon as you stop working or lose your current employer coverage (even if you sign up for COBRA or retiree health coverage from your employer). You have eight months to enroll in Medicare once you stop working OR your employer coverage ends (whichever happens first), but you will want to plan ahead and contact Social Security before your employer coverage ends so you do not have a gap in coverage.

! WARNING ! If you do not enroll in Part B within eight months of losing your coverage based on current employment, you may have to pay **a lifetime late enrollment penalty**. In addition, you will only be able to enroll during the Medicare General Enrollment Period, from January 1 to March 31 each year, and your coverage will not start until July 1. This may cause a gap in your coverage.

If neither you nor your spouse is still working, and thus you have no employer coverage, and you failed to enroll in Part B during your seven-month Initial Enrollment Period, you will have to wait until the Medicare General Enrollment Period, from January 1 to March 31 each year. If you enroll during this period, your coverage begins on July 1.

! WARNING ! If you do not have other coverage and you do not enroll in Part B during your Initial Enrollment Period, you may have to pay **a lifetime late enrollment penalty** for Part B. For Part B, the penalty is a 10% increase in your monthly premium for every 12-month period you were eligible for Part B but did not have Part B. You will have to pay the Part B penalty monthly for as long as you have Part B coverage.

How and when can I enroll in a Medicare Advantage plan?

After close consideration of the Medicare Advantage plan,

if you are ready to enroll in this type of plan, what do you need to know? First and foremost, you must verify that you are in the Medicare Advantage plan's service area and whether your doctors and hospital accept this plan. This can be done by calling an individual insurance agent, calling the plan company directly, or going online with the selected company. At no time should you call your doctor's office directly to confirm whether your doctor accepts this plan. The reason for this is that you might inadequately describe the plan you are enrolling in and find out afterwards that the doctor does not take this plan.

Medicare Advantage plans must enroll any eligible beneficiary who applies regardless of health status. Starting January 2021, individuals with ESRD can choose either Original Medicare or a Medicare Advantage Plan when deciding how to get Medicare coverage.

Special Needs Plans (SNPs) must limit new enrollments to beneficiaries who meet specified plan eligibility criteria (e.g., beneficiaries who are dual eligible, have specified chronic conditions (which may include ESRD), or reside in institutions or live in the community but require an institutional level of care). Medicare SNPs tailor their benefits, provider choices, and drug formularies to best meet the specific needs of the groups they serve.

Medicare Advantage plans have a limited time for enrollment. Signing up late can affect your cost and can affect the effective date of the policy. There are three times when you can sign up for a Medicare Advantage plan:

- During your Initial Enrollment Period when you first become eligible for Medicare or when you turn age 65;

- During certain enrollment periods that occur each year;
- Under certain circumstances that qualify you for a Special Enrollment Period (SEP), such as:

1. You move
2. You become eligible for Medicaid
3. You qualify for Extra Help with Medicare prescription drug costs
4. You are getting care in an institution, such as a skilled nursing facility or long-term care hospital
5. You want to switch to a plan with a five-star overall quality rating. (Quality ratings are available on Medicare.gov.)

How can I decide whether to enroll in Medicare Part A and Part B when I turn age 65?

As you approach age 65, Medicare lurks around the next corner waiting to catch you off guard. Understanding what is ahead will help you make the right decisions which can shape your future health care needs. The following information will help you select the path to Medicare that best suits your individual needs.

Timing might not be everything, but it is very important when it comes to Medicare. The first time you can enroll in Medicare is called your "Initial Enrollment Period." Your seven-month Initial Enrollment Period usually begins three months before the month you turn age 65, includes the month you turn age 65, and ends three months after the month you turn age 65. Your decision as to whether to enroll in Part A and Part B during the Initial Enrollment Period should be made at least three months before you turn age 65. (See Charts & Data—Chart # 4)

Medicare Part A is sometimes called "Hospital Insurance." Part A helps cover inpatient hospital care, skilled nursing facility care, hospice care, and home health care. Most people should enroll in Medicare Part A when they turn age 65, even if they have health insurance from an employer. This is because most people paid Medicare taxes while they worked and therefore do not pay a monthly premium for Part A. However, some people, such as people who contribute to a Health Savings Account (HSA) or those who must pay a premium for Part A, may want to consider delaying Medicare Part A until a later date.

Medicare Part B is sometimes called "Medical Insurance." It helps cover services from doctors and other health care providers, outpatient care, home health care, durable medical equipment, and some preventive services, including certain vaccines and cancer screenings. Most people need to enroll in Part B when they turn age 65. Only people who have health insurance from their (or their spouse's) current employer may be able to delay enrolling in Part B.

Medicare premiums vary depending on how long you (or your spouse) worked prior to initially signing up for Medicare and your current income. Most people do NOT pay a monthly premium for Part A. If you (or your spouse) worked and paid Medicare taxes for long enough (usually about ten years), you would not have to pay a premium for Part A. This is called "premium-free Part A." If you did not pay Medicare taxes long enough, you can still get Part A but you may have to pay a monthly premium. This is called "premium Part A."

Everyone pays a monthly premium for Part B. The premium varies depending on your income and when you enroll in Part B. Most people will pay the standard premium amount which is currently $164.90 per month.

Author's Insights and Conclusion

A change is in sight. The intention is to move forward. Initial Enrollment Period is just around the corner. Now I know how to enroll and what is needed to meet the requirements of the Centers of Medicare and Medicaid. Jimmy Dean once said, "I can't change the direction of the wind, but I can adjust my sails to always reach my destination." With the right tools in hand, you can make it to where you are going.

STAGE FOUR

ACTION

Introduction

I now know where I am going, and it is time to modify my insurance coverage. Timing is very important. I need to understand just what Medicare is going to cost so there will be no financial surprises.

Initial Enrollment Period

If you sign up for Part A and/or Part B during the first three months of your Initial Enrollment Period, in most cases your coverage starts the first day of your birthday month. However, if your birthday is on the first day of the month, your coverage will start the first day of the prior month. (See Charts & Data—Chart # 4)

If you are nearing age 65, but not receiving Social Security or Railroad Retirement Board (RRB) benefits, you will need to sign up for Medicare. You may sign up for Parts A and B during your Initial Enrollment Period, which begins three months before your 65th birthday, includes the month you turn age 65 and ends three months after you turn age 65. Contact Social Security to sign up by visiting your local Social Security Office or going online.

If you enroll in Part A and/or Part B the month you turn age 65 or during the last three months of your Initial Enrollment Period, the effective date for your Medicare coverage will be the first day of the month following the month you sign up.

If you join a Medicare Advantage plan for the first time, and you are not satisfied with the plan, you will have special rights under federal law to purchase a Medigap policy if you return to Original Medicare within 12 months of joining. If you had a Medigap policy before you joined, you may be able to obtain the same policy again if the company still sells it. If it is not available, you can purchase another Medigap policy. If you joined a Medicare Advantage plan when you were first eligible for Medicare, you can choose from any Medigap policy within the first year of joining. You may be able to join a Medicare Prescription Drug Plan. Some states provide additional special rights.

The best time to purchase a Medigap policy is during your Medigap Open Enrollment period. This six-month period begins on the first day of the month in which you are age 65 or older and enrolled in Part B. (Some states have additional Open Enrollment Periods.) After this enrollment period, you may not be able to purchase a Medigap policy. If you can purchase one, it may be more expensive.

If you delay enrolling in Part B because you have group health coverage based on your (or your spouse's) current employment, your Medigap Open Enrollment Period will not start until you sign up for Part B.

If you are on disability for 24 months, you are then eligible for Medicare and can sign up on the 25th month.

Special Enrollment Periods

In most cases, you must stay enrolled for the calendar year starting the date your coverage begins; however, in certain situations, you may be able to join, change, or drop a Medicare Advantage plan during a Special Enrollment Period. Some examples are: you move out of your plan's service area; you have Medicaid; you qualify for Extra Help; or you reside in an institution (such as a nursing home).

Why do they need more of my money?

Do you ever feel like the federal government cannot get enough of your money? They always seem to be digging deeper into your pocket, asking for more. Well, here is their explanation for your increased premium.

Part B helps pay for your doctors' services and outpatient care. It also covers other medical services, such as physical and occupational therapy, and some home health care. For most beneficiaries, the government pays a substantial portion—about 75 percent—of the Part B premium, and the beneficiary pays the remaining 25 percent.

If you are a higher income beneficiary (five percent of the population), you will bear a greater responsibility for this cost and will pay a larger percentage of the total cost of the Part B premium. In addition to a monthly premium, an assessment will be made by the Internal Revenue Service (IRS) to determine the extra amount to be paid—an amount that is equal to 35, 50, 65, or 80 percent of the total cost of the Part B premium. This determination is made by the Social Security Administration and is based on the income reported to the IRS by the beneficiary on the most recent federal income tax return provided by the IRS. In addition, this same principle is applicable to prescription drug coverage. Most beneficiaries only pay a portion of the overall cost for their medications, leaving the government to pay the remainder.

For more information on this issue please refer to *Medicare and You 2023*.

How does Social Security determine if I must pay higher premiums?

To determine if higher premiums are due, the Social Security Administration uses the most recent federal income tax return provided by the Internal Revenue Service (IRS). A sliding scale based on your modified adjusted gross income (MAGI) is used to make the adjustment. Your MAGI is your total adjusted gross income and tax-exempt interest income.

Pursuant to current regulations, the following persons will pay higher premiums for Part B and Medicare prescription drug coverage: (See Appendix—Chart # 5)

- A married couple, filing jointly, with a MAGI greater than $194,000.00
- A single person with a MAGI greater than $97,000.00

(See chart on Social Security.Gov/HI 01101.020 IRMAA Sliding Scale Tables)

If the IRS determines that your MAGI is in one of these categories, you will receive a letter from the Social Security Administration notifying you and giving you the reason for their decision.

As stated above, the Social Security Administration uses the most recent federal income tax return that the IRS provides. In some cases, this might be a tax return from two years back. If a more recent tax return has been filed and was not used, and that tax return reflects a change in your income amount, you may call or visit any local Social Security Office to have your records updated. If there has been an amendment to your tax return which changes your income amount, you should contact your local Social Security Office as well. You must have a copy of the amended tax return which was filed and your acknowledgment receipt from the IRS.

Adjustments can be made if new information is available that makes a difference in your income level. Such items would include:

- You married, divorced, or became widowed
- You or your spouse stopped working or reduced your work hours
- You or your spouse lost income-producing property because of a disaster or other event beyond your control
- You or your spouse experienced a scheduled cessation, termination, or reorganization of an employer's pension plan
- You or your spouse received a settlement from an employer or former employer because of the employer's closure, bankruptcy, or reorganization

Documentation verifying the event and the reduction in your income will be required and could include a death certificate, a letter from your employer regarding your retirement, or something similar. If you filed a federal income tax return for the year in question, you will need to provide a signed copy of the return.

Use Form SSA-44 Medicare Income-Related Monthly Adjustment Amount – Life-Changing Event to report a major life-changing event. If your income has decreased, you may also use Form SSA-44 to request a reduction in your income-related monthly adjustment amount. Form SSA-44 may be found online at www.socialsecurity.gov/forms/ssa-44. pdf

Is help available for individuals with limited income?

There are many misconceptions regarding Medicare. One such fallacy is that Medicare is a free service provided to all American citizens age 65 and older. On the contrary, Medicare can be quite expensive. So, what is a person to do if he or she has limited income?

There are four kinds of Medicare Savings Programs:
- Qualified Medicare Beneficiary (QMB) Program
- Specified Low-Income Medicare Beneficiary (SLMB) Program
- Qualifying Individual (QI) Program
- Qualified Disabled and Working Individuals (QDWI) Program

In most cases, to qualify for a Medicare Savings Program, you must have income and resources below a certain limit. Many states figure your income and resources differently so you should check with your state to see if you qualify. Call or visit your Medicaid office and ask for information regarding Medicare Savings Programs. Visit Medicare.gov/contacts to determine the telephone number for your state. You can also call 800-MEDICARE (800-633-4227). TTY users can call 877-486-2048.

Beneficiaries may qualify for help from their state to pay the Medicare Part A (if any) and Part B premiums, the Part A and Part B deductibles and cost sharing, and/or some Part D prescription drug costs.

There are other programs available to assist in the high cost of Medicare:

- State Pharmacy Assistance Programs (SPAPs)
- Pharmaceutical Assistance Programs (also called Patient Assistance Programs)
- Programs of All-inclusive Care for the Elderly (PACE)
- Supplemental Security Income (SSI) benefits

You can visit benefits.gov/ssa and use the "Benefit Eligibility Screening Tool" to find out if you are eligible for SSI or other benefits. Call Social Security at 800-772-1213 or contact your local Social Security Office for more information. TTY users can call 800-325-0778.

1. Single person - income less than $21,870.00 and resources less than $16,600.00 per year
2. Married person living with a spouse and no other dependents - income less than $29,580.00 and resources less than $33,240.00 per year

What are the income limits for Medicare Extra Help for 2023?

Extra Help is a Medicare program to help people with limited income and resources to pay Medicare prescription drug costs. You may qualify for Extra Help if your yearly income and resources are below these limits in 2023: https://www.medicare.gov/your-medicare-costs/get-help-paying-costs/lower-prescription-costs

You may automatically qualify for Extra Help, and if so, Medicare will mail you a letter advising you if you qualify. You do not need to apply for Extra Help if you get this letter.

If you receive this letter, you should follow the instructions in the letter regarding qualifying for Extra Help.

There are some parameters to qualify for the program, mostly related to income and assets. The government has updated the income limits for 2023, which—per Medicare Interactive—are now: up to $1,719 monthly income for individuals; up to $2,309 monthly income for married couples.

I have been considered disabled for two years this fall. Does this qualify me for Medicare?

I have been considered disabled for two years this fall. Is it true that even though I am not age 65, I can still receive Medicare benefits?

If you are an individual with disabilities who is under age 65, you will automatically receive Part A and Part B after you receive disability benefits from Social Security or certain disability benefits from the Railroad Board (RRB) for 24 months. Under these circumstances, you will receive your Medicare card (Red, White, and Blue card) in the mail approximately three months before your 25th month of disability benefits. If you do nothing, you will keep Part B and will pay Part B premiums.

If your disability is based on a diagnosis of ALS (Amyotrophic Lateral Sclerosis, also called Lou Gehrig's disease), you will get Part A and Part B automatically the month your Social Security disability benefits begin.

If your disability is End-Stage Renal Disease (ESRD) and you want to receive Medicare benefits, you will need to sign up. If your disability is ESRD, you should contact the Social

Security Administration to find out when and how to sign up for Part A and Part B.

You also are given an opportunity to refuse Part B coverage. If you did not sign up for Part B (or Part A if you must buy it) when you were first eligible because you were covered under a group health plan based on current employment (your own, a spouse's, or if you are disabled, a family member's), you can sign up for Part A and/or Part B:

■ Any time you are still covered by the group health plan

■ During the eight-month period that begins the month after the employment ends or the coverage ends, whichever happens first

NOTE: Disabled individuals who live in Puerto Rico automatically get Part A after 24 months but need to sign up for Part B if they want it.

What is a Special Needs Plan?

A Special Needs Plan (SNP) is a Medicare Advantage (MA) coordinated care plan (CCP) specifically designed to provide targeted care and limit enrollment to special needs individuals. A special needs individual could be any one of the following:

1. An institutionalized individual
2. A dual eligible (Medicare and Medicaid) individual
3. An individual with a severe or disabling chronic condition, as specified by the Centers for Medicare and Medicaid Services (CMS)

SNP plans come in various packages of MA CCP plans. This could include either a local or regional preferred provider organization (i.e., LPPO or RPPO) plan, a health maintenance organization (HMO) plan, or an HMO Point-of-Service (HMO-POS) plan. CMS has established three different types of SNPs:

1. Chronic Condition SNP (C-SNP)
2. Dual Eligible SNP (D-SNP)
3. Institutional SNP (I-SNP)

All SNPs must provide Part D prescription drug coverage since special needs individuals must have access to prescription drugs to manage and control their special health care needs.

Chronic Condition Special Needs Plans (C-SNPs) are SNPs that restrict enrollment to special needs individuals with specific severe or disabling chronic conditions. By definition, special needs individuals with severe or disabling chronic conditions are special needs individuals "who have one or more co-morbid and medically complex chronic conditions that are substantially disabling or life threatening; have a high risk of hospitalization or other significant adverse health outcomes; and require specialized delivery systems across domains of care."

Three federal agencies—the Agency for Healthcare Research and Quality (AHRQ), the Centers for Disease Control and Prevention (CDC), and Centers for Medicare and Medicaid Services (CMS)—have proposed a list of SNP-specific chronic conditions. (See Charts & Data—Chart # 8)

When completing the SNP application, MAOs may apply

to offer a C-SNP that targets any one of the following:

- A single CMS-approved chronic condition (shown in Chart # 8)
- A CMS-approved group of commonly co-morbid and clinically-linked conditions (described herein), or
- A MAO-customized group of multiple chronic conditions (described herein)

CMS accepts applications for C-SNPs that focus on the following multi-condition groupings:

- **Group 1: Diabetes mellitus and chronic heart failure**
- **Group 2: Chronic heart failure and cardiovascular disorders**
- **Group 3:** Diabetes mellitus and cardiovascular disorders
- **Group 4: Diabetes mellitus, chronic heart failure, and cardiovascular disorders and**
- **Group 5: Stroke and cardiovascular disorders**

Dual Eligible Special Needs Plans (D-SNPs) enroll individuals who are entitled to both Medicare (Title XVIII) and medical assistance from a state plan under Medicaid (Title XIX). The Medicaid eligibility categories encompass all categories of Medicaid eligibility including:

- Full Medicaid (only)
- Qualified Medicare Beneficiary without other Medicaid (QMB only)
- QMB Plus
- Specified Low-Income Medicare Beneficiary without other Medicaid (SLMB only)
- SLMB Plus
- Qualifying Individual (QI) and

- Qualified Disabled and Working Individual (QDWI)

States may vary in the eligibility requirements for each category, so it is important that the specific state requirements be considered.

Institutional Special Needs Plans (I-SNPs), are SNPs that restrict enrollment to MA eligible individuals who, for 90 days or longer, have had or are expected to need, the level of services provided in a long-term care facility, a skilled nursing facility, a long-term care nursing facility, an intermediate care facility for individuals with intellectual disabilities, or an inpatient psychiatric facility.

Every SNP must have a Model of Care (MOC) approved by the National Committee for Quality Assurance (NCQA). The MOC provides the basic outline under which the SNP will meet the needs of each of its enrollees. The MOC is an important quality improvement tool and essential component for guaranteeing that the unique needs of each enrollee are recognized by the SNP and addressed through the Plan's care management practices. The MOC provides the substance for promoting SNP quality, care management, and care harmonization processes. The MOC must meet an approval process which if passed, will grant them a one, two, or three-year period of operation.

I love to travel. Can my Medicare plan travel with me?

Travel is a dream many have as they enter their retirement years. Most plans try to accommodate for these anticipated adventures. There is a wide spectrum among the Medicare policies offered.

Original Medicare allows you to see any doctor that accepts Medicare and is taking new patients anywhere in the United States.

Medicare Advantage plans (Part C) work within a network of doctors. Preferred Provider Organizations (PPO) and Health Maintenance Organizations (HMO) are the two network groups available. Within these two network groups are the individual insurance companies. Each insurance company may market both PPO and HMO plans. The benefits under each plan can be quite different.

The next bit of information to be noted is generally the way the network functions in the subject matter. PPOs are generally more flexible on the issue of travel. They are accepted in states in addition to the one in which the policy was written. You are subject to the criteria we spoke of before—does the doctor accept Medicare and is the doctor taking new patients. In addition to these two criteria, now you must ask if the doctor is in the plan network. HMOs are more restrictive. I often refer to them as being territorial because they generally are not accepted outside the state in which they were written. Some HMO plans also restrict the use to specific counties within the state.

All network plans include a provision for emergency care while traveling. If you are having an emergency, go to the nearest hospital for treatment. Some HMO plans are allowing an option when traveling out of state to call the phone number on the back of your plan card and let them know where you will be on your trip, and they will let you know if there are any doctors who might accept the terms of the contract.

Original Medicare does not provide for benefits while

traveling abroad. Most Medicare Advantage plans do provide this benefit. Medicare Supplement plans make provisions for medically necessary emergency care services during the first 60 days of each trip outside of the United States. You should note that this is for emergency care only. The foreign travel benefit pays 80% of charges after a $250.00 deductible, with up to a $50,000.00 lifetime maximum. This benefit is reimbursable. A Medicare Advantage plan covers care outside of the United States, it is only for medically necessary emergency care and there is a co-pay you will have to pay. This co-pay may not be waived if you are admitted to the hospital.

What is the Part D late enrollment penalty?

The late enrollment penalty is an amount that is added to your Part D premium. You may owe a late enrollment penalty if at any time after your Initial Enrollment Period is over, there is a period of 63 or more days in a row when you do not have Part D or other creditable prescription drug coverage. You will generally have to pay the penalty for as long as you have Part D coverage.

NOTE: If you receive Extra Help, you do not pay a late enrollment penalty.

If you retire or otherwise lose employer/union creditable coverage and join a Medicare Part D plan or otherwise obtain creditable drug coverage within 63 days, there will not be a late enrollment penalty.

Medicare health and prescription drug plans can decide

not to participate in Medicare for the coming year. In these cases, your coverage under the plan will end after December 31. Your plan will send you a letter regarding your options before Open Enrollment. If this happens you can choose another plan during the Medicare Annual Election between October 15–December 7. Your coverage will begin January 1. You will have the right to purchase certain Medigap policies within 63 days after your plan coverage ends.

Author's Insights and Conclusion

Bertolt Brecht well said, "Because things are the way they are, things will not stay the way they are." We would not expect an infant to remain the size they were at birth, we await change. If I do not embrace change, I will be left behind. Life changes so fast, and something changes every day. So be ready to act or else be left behind.

What the journey costs is of great concern to most people. There are those who will have to pay more than others for the same services just because their past income has exceeded the norm. There are others that have a lower income than the norm, so decisions must be made. Others may have been grouped in the category of Special Needs due to a health issue they have, so plans might be to move away from the traditional Medicare and elect a plan that meets your needs.

MAINTENANCE FOR MEDICARE

The First Year and Beyond

Introduction

The world we live in is evolving even as you are reading this book. In our country, our parents and grandparents' main way of travel was by horse. New discoveries led to new ways to travel—A-Models, single-engine planes, railroads. As technology advanced it was clear that we could not remain as we were. Without the changing of seasons, we would not have adequate growing and harvesting time.

When taking a journey in Medicare, you should always be prepared for adjustments. Medicines change, doctors change, and plans change. Sometimes you may need to make a change to save money, and you know prices will increase. **When** these events occur, consult your insurance agent to learn what your options are. This last Unit is all about maintenance, and sometimes that means we need to change things. What you can do, when you can do it, and how you make changes is an important part of maintenance.

Am I locked in, or can I change my mind?

Why would you elect to change from the Medigap policy you have currently to another policy? You may be paying for benefits you do not need, or you may need benefits that your current policy does not provide. Sometimes you have what you need but would like to change companies. This may be because the current premiums are more expensive and the new company's premiums are less expensive.

Now that we have considered why you may desire to make a change in policies, we should determine if you can make a change. Federal law makes this point very clear—if you are within your six-month Medigap open enrollment period or if you are eligible under a specific circumstance or guaranteed issue rights, you may make a change. **You do not have to wait a certain length of time after buying your first Medigap policy before you can switch to a different Medigap policy.**

Federal law provides the situations set forth below for switching Medigap policies:

• You have an older Medigap policy.

You do not have to switch. If you choose a newer Medigap policy, you must give up the older policy (except for your 30-day "free look period"). Remember that with the new policy, some of the coverage from the older policy might not carry over.

• You have had your old Medigap policy for less than six months, and you have a pre-existing condition.

The Medigap insurance company may choose to make you wait up to six months for coverage of pre-existing conditions. The number of months you have had your current Medigap policy must be subtracted from the time you must wait before your new Medigap policy covers your pre-existing condition.

• You have had your old Medigap policy for six months or more and that policy has the same benefits as your new policy.

The new insurance company cannot exclude your pre-existing condition. If you have had the current Medigap policy for less than six months, the number of months will be deducted from the waiting period the new policy imposes for your pre-existing condition.

- The new Medigap policy has a different benefit that is not in your current Medigap policy.

There could still be a six-month waiting period for that benefit to be covered.

- You are moving out of the state.

Medigap plans are not territorial and can be used throughout the United States, so you do not have to change plans. If you decide to change plans, you may have to pay more for your new Medigap policy.

- You have a Medicare SELECT policy, and you are moving out of the policy area for that policy.

You have the following choices:
Buy a standardized Medigap policy from your current Medigap policy insurance company that offers the same or fewer benefits than your current Medicare SELECT policy. If you have had your Medicare SELECT policy for more than six months, you will not have to answer any medical questions and will receive a guaranteed issue. If you choose to use your guaranteed issue to purchase Medigap plans, you

are limited to Medigap Plans A, B, C, F, K, or L. These are sold by insurance companies that are licensed to do business in your state. People eligible for Medicare on or after January 1, 2020 have the right to buy Plans D and G instead of Plans C and F.

- You are joining a Medicare Advantage plan.

Medigap policies and Medicare Advantage policies do not work together. You must drop your Medigap plan, and if you have a stand-alone prescription drug plan, it too must be canceled to add on an Advantage plan. You should speak with your insurance company to verify your right to make a change and the time that any change can be completed before you drop any plan.

It is important to call the new insurance company and arrange to apply for your new Medigap policy if you elect to change insurance companies. If your new application is accepted, then you should call your current insurance company and ask for your coverage to end. The insurance company will tell you how to submit a request to end your coverage.

Medicare offers a free-look period for the first 30 days after you get your new policy. In this 30-day period, you will have to pay the premiums for both policies. Remember, do not cancel your first Medigap policy until you have decided to keep the second Medigap policy. You must state on the new application that you are cancelling the first policy. Once you have verified the second policy is in force, you must cancel the previous policy.

Once the six month look back period is over, am I locked in to my current plan?

Is my plan right for me? Can I make any changes? First, consider why someone would want to make a change beyond the "free look period". Let's face it—things change. Sometimes you might find that the plan you are on costs too much. This could be because of the premium, maybe your plan no longer has one of your medicines on the formulary, perhaps your co-pays are too high, or your maximum out-of-pocket expense worries you. Doctors have been known to drop a plan in mid-stream, leaving you with a decision to change doctors or change plans. Unfortunately, a plan might not measure up to the quality of services you desire. All of these, and maybe more, are reasons that you may elect to change plans. Oh, yes, I did not mention that you may have an Advantage plan that is just not working out, so you would like to go back to a Supplement plan.

Good news, changes can be made but **ONLY during the Annual Election Period (AEP), which runs from October 15 to December 7 each year**.

What changes can you make during the AEP?

- Change to a Medicare Advantage plan from Original Medicare, Part A and Part B
- Change from a Medicare Advantage plan to Original Medicare, Part A and Part B
- Change from one Medicare Advantage plan to another (regardless of whether either plan offers drug coverage).

The insured must have "credible coverage" from some other source, or they may pay a penalty for not attaining Part D coverage

- Enroll in a Part D prescription drug plan
- Change from one Medicare prescription drug plan to another
- Opt out of Medicare prescription drug coverage completely

Changes you make during the AEP go into effect January 1 of the next year. If you are satisfied that your current coverage will meet your needs for next year, **you do not need to do anything**. You may make more than one enrollment choice during the Annual Election Period, but the last one made prior to the end of the Annual Election Period, as determined by the date the plan or marketing representative receives the completed enrollment form, will be the election that takes effect.

You should decide which plan will meet your needs for next year. If you want to change plans, call the plan you want to join or your agent. Medicare can also help you enroll online, in person, or on the telephone. Remember, during Medicare's Annual Enrollment Period (AEP), you can decide to stay in Original Medicare or join a Medicare Advantage plan (such as an HMO or PPO). If you are already in a Medicare Advantage plan, you can use AEP to switch back to Original Medicare.

Also, you should keep in mind that Medicare plans can change each year.

Important Medicare dates

September & October - Review and Compare

- **Review:** Your plan may be changing. Review any notices from your plan about changes for next year.
- **Compare**: Starting in October, use Medicare's Plan Finder or meet with your agent to find a plan that meets your needs. Visit the Medicare Plan Finder at Medicare.gov/find-a-plan.

October 15 - Annual Election Period begins

This is the one time of year when ALL individuals with Medicare can make changes to their health and prescription drug plans for the next year.
- **Decide**: October 15 is the first day you can change your Medicare coverage for next year.

December 7 - Annual Election Period ends

- In most cases, **December 7** is the last day you can change your Medicare coverage for next year. The plan must receive your enrollment request (application) by midnight on **December 7.**

January 1 - Coverage begins

Your new coverage begins **January 1** if you switch to a new plan. If you stay with the same plan, any changes to coverage, benefits, or costs for the new year will begin on January 1.

Medicare Advantage Open Enrollment Period. (OEP)

- **From January 1 – March 31 each year,** if you are enrolled in a Medicare Advantage plan, you can switch to a different Medicare Advantage Plan or switch to Original Medicare (and join a separate Medicare drug plan) once during this time.
- Visit www.**Medicare.gov** or call **1-800-MEDICARE** (1-800-633-4227) to learn more. TTY users can call 1-877-486-2048.

5-star Special Enrollment Period: You can change to a Medicare Advantage plan or Medicare Cost plan that has five stars for its overall star rating from December 8–November 30 each year. You can only use this Special Enrollment Period once during this time frame. The overall star ratings are available at Medicare.gov/find-a-plan.

General Enrollment Period: If you did not sign up for Part A (if you must purchase it) and/or Part B (for which you must pay premiums) during your Initial Enrollment Period, and you do not qualify for a Special Enrollment Period, you can sign up between January 1–March 31 each year. Your coverage will start the month after you sign up, and you may have to pay a higher Part A and/or Part B premium for late enrollment. If you obtain Part B for the first time during the General Enrollment Period, you can also join a Medicare drug plan from April 1–June 30. Your coverage starts the month after you sign up.

Author's Insights and Conclusion

Earlier we quoted Heraclitus as saying, "change is the only constant in life." This simply means that the world is always changing, and so are people, along with their needs. Medicare is not a dark pit that one drives off into never to be heard from again. Sure, there are potholes to avoid along the way, but all of these can be avoided if you take caution, ask for help, and prepare ahead of time. There will be times when the best thing to do is make changes in your course. Medicare allows "The Free Look Period" to make any necessary changes to your Medigap plan to improve your pathway. The Annual Election Period is made available for those who may have encountered a disruption in their Medicare pursuits.

Always consult your insurance agent to receive assistance in these and all matters regarding Medicare. Do not forget AEP is October 15–December 7 each year and remember to bring your updated drug list—it can save you money!

What key Medicare terms do I need to know?

Appeal - An appeal is the action you can take if you disagree with a coverage or payment decision made by Medicare, your Medicare health plan, or your Medicare Prescription Drug Plan. You can appeal if Medicare or your plan denies one of these:
- Your request for a health care service, supply, item, or prescription drug that you think you should be able to get
- Your request for payment of a health care service, supply, item, or prescription drug you have already received
- Your request to change the amount you must pay for a health care service, supply, item, or prescription drug

You can also appeal if Medicare or your plan stops providing or paying for all or part of a health care service, supply, item, or prescription drug you think you still need.

Assignment - An agreement by your doctor, provider, or supplier to be paid directly by Medicare, to accept the payment amount Medicare approves for the service, and to not bill you for any more than the Medicare deductible and coinsurance.

Benefit period - The way that Original Medicare measures your use of hospital and skilled nursing facility (SNF) services. A benefit period begins the day you are admitted as an inpatient in a hospital or SNF. The benefit period ends when you have not received any inpatient hospital care (or skilled care in a SNF) for 60 days in a row. If you go into a hospital or a SNF after one benefit period has ended, a new benefit period begins. You must pay the inpatient hospital deductible for each benefit period. There is no limit to the number of benefit periods.

Coinsurance - An amount you may be required to pay as your share of the cost of services after you pay any deductibles. Coinsurance is usually a percentage (for example, 20%).

Co-payment - An amount you may be required to pay as your share of the cost for a medical service or supply, such as a doctor's visit, hospital outpatient visit, or prescription drug. A co-payment is usually a set amount, rather than a percentage. For example, you might pay $10 or $20 for a doctor's visit or prescription drug.

Creditable prescription drug coverage - Prescription drug coverage (for example, from an employer or union) that is expected to pay, on average, at least as much as Medicare's standard prescription drug coverage. People who have this kind of coverage when they become eligible for Medicare can generally keep that coverage without paying a penalty if they decide to enroll in Medicare prescription drug coverage later.

Critical access hospital - A small facility that provides outpatient services, as well as inpatient services on a limited basis, to people in rural areas.

Custodial care - Non-skilled personal care, such as assistance with activities of daily living such as bathing, dressing, eating, getting in or out of a bed or chair, moving around, and using the bathroom. It may also include the kind of health-related care that most people do themselves, such as using eye drops. In most cases, Medicare does not pay for custodial care.

Deductible - The amount you must pay for health care or prescriptions before Original Medicare, your prescription drug plan, or your other insurance begins to pay.

Demonstrations - Special projects, sometimes called "pilot programs" or "research studies," that test improvements in Medicare coverage, payment, and quality of care. They usually operate only for a limited time, for a specific group of people, and in specific areas.

Exception - A type of Medicare prescription drug coverage determination. A formulary exception is a drug plan's decision to cover a drug that is not on its drug list or to waive a coverage rule. A tiering exception is a drug plan's decision to charge a lower amount for a drug that is on its non-preferred drug tier. You or your prescriber must request an exception, and your doctor or other prescriber must provide a supporting statement explaining the medical reason for the exception.

Extra Help - A Medicare program to help people with limited income and resources pay Medicare prescription drug program costs, such as premiums, deductibles, and coinsurance.

Formulary - A list of prescription drugs covered by a prescription drug plan or another insurance plan offering prescription drug benefits. Also called a drug list.

Inpatient rehabilitation facility - A hospital, or part of a hospital, that provides an intensive rehabilitation program to inpatients.

Institution - For the purposes of this publication, an institution is a facility that provides short-term or long-term care, such as a nursing home, skilled nursing facility (SNF), or rehabilitation hospital. Private residences, such as an assisted living facility or group home, are not considered institutions for this purpose.

Lifetime reserve days - In Original Medicare, these are additional days that Medicare will pay for when you are in a hospital for more than 90 days. You have a total of 60 reserve days that can be used during your lifetime. For each lifetime reserve day, Medicare pays all covered costs except for a daily coinsurance.

Long-term care hospital – An acute care hospital that provides treatment for patients who stay, on average, more than 25 days. Most patients are transferred here from an intensive or critical care unit. Services provided include comprehensive rehabilitation, respiratory therapy, head trauma treatment, and pain management.

Medically necessary - Health care services or supplies needed to diagnose or treat an illness, injury, condition, disease, or its symptoms and that meet accepted standards of medicine.

Medicare Advantage Plan (Part C) - A type of Medicare health plan offered by a private company that contracts with Medicare to provide Part A and Part B benefits. Medicare Advantage plans include Health Maintenance Organizations, Preferred Provider Organizations, Private Fee-for-Service Plans, Special Needs Plans, and Medicare Medical Savings Account Plans. If you are enrolled in a Medicare Advantage plan, most Medicare services are covered through the plan and are not paid for under Original Medicare. Most Medicare Advantage plans offer prescription drug coverage.

Medicare-approved amount - In Original Medicare, this is the amount a doctor or supplier who accepts assignment can be paid. It may be less than the actual amount a doctor or supplier charges. Medicare pays part of this amount, and you are responsible for the difference.

Medicare health plan - Generally, a plan offered by a

private company that contracts with Medicare to provide Part A and Part B benefits to people with Medicare who enroll in the plan. Medicare health plans include all Medicare Advantage plans, Medicare Cost Plans, and Demonstration/Pilot Programs. Programs of All-inclusive Care for the Elderly (PACE) organizations are special types of Medicare health plans. PACE plans can be offered by public or private entities and provide Part D and other benefits in addition to Part A and Part B benefits.

Medicare Part A (Hospital Insurance) - Part A covers inpatient hospital stays, care in a skilled nursing facility, hospice care, and some home health care.

Medicare Part B (Medical Insurance) - Part B covers certain doctors' services, outpatient care, medical supplies, and preventive services.

Medicare plan - Any plan other than Original Medicare through which you can get your Medicare health or prescription drug coverage. This term includes all Medicare health plans and Medicare Prescription Drug Plans.

Medicare prescription drug coverage (Part D) - Optional benefits for prescription drugs available to all people with Medicare for an additional charge. This coverage is offered by insurance companies and other private companies approved by Medicare.

Medicare Prescription Drug Plan (Part D) - Part D adds prescription drug coverage to Original Medicare, some Medicare Cost plans, some Medicare Private-Fee-for-Service plans, and Medicare Medical Savings Account plans. These plans are offered by insurance companies and other private companies approved by Medicare. Medicare Advantage plans may also offer prescription drug coverage that follows the same rules as Medicare Prescription Drug plans.

Medigap Open Enrollment Period – A one-time-only, six-month period when federal law allows you to purchase any Medigap policy you want that is sold in your state. It begins in the first month that you are covered under Medicare Part B, and you are age 65 or older. During this period, you cannot be denied a Medigap policy or charged more due to past or present health problems. Some states may have additional Open Enrollment rights under state law.

Medigap policy - Medicare supplement insurance sold by private insurance companies to fill "gaps" in Original Medicare coverage.

Original Medicare - Original Medicare is a fee-for-service health plan that has two parts: Part A (Hospital Insurance) and Part B (Medical Insurance). After you pay a deductible, Medicare pays its share of the Medicare-approved amount, and you pay your share (coinsurance and deductibles).

Premium - The periodic payment to Medicare, an insurance company, or a health care plan for health or prescription drug coverage.

Preventive services - Health care to prevent illness or detect illness at an early stage, when treatment is likely to work best (for example, preventive services include Pap tests, flu shots, and screening mammograms).

Primary care doctor - The doctor you see first for most health problems. He or she makes sure you get the care you need to keep you healthy. He or she also may talk with other doctors and health care providers about your care and refer you to them. In many Medicare Advantage plans, you must see your primary care doctor before you see any other health care provider.

Referral - A written order from your primary care doctor for you to see a specialist or get certain medical services. In many Health Maintenance Organizations (HMOs), you need to have a referral before you can receive medical care from anyone except your primary care doctor. If you do not get a referral first, the plan may not pay for the services.

Service area - A geographic area where a health insurance plan accepts members if it limits membership based on where people live. For plans that limit which doctors and hospitals you may use, it is also generally the area where you can get routine (non-emergency) services. The plan may disenroll you if you move out of the plan's service area.

Skilled nursing facility (SNF) care - Skilled nursing care and rehabilitation services provided daily in a skilled nursing facility.

State Health Insurance Assistance Program (SHIP) - A state program that receives money from the federal government to give free local health insurance counseling to people with Medicare.

State Medical Assistance (Medicaid) office - A state or local agency that can give information about, and help with applications for, Medicaid programs that help pay medical bills for people with limited income and resources.

CHARTS & DATA

Chart # 1

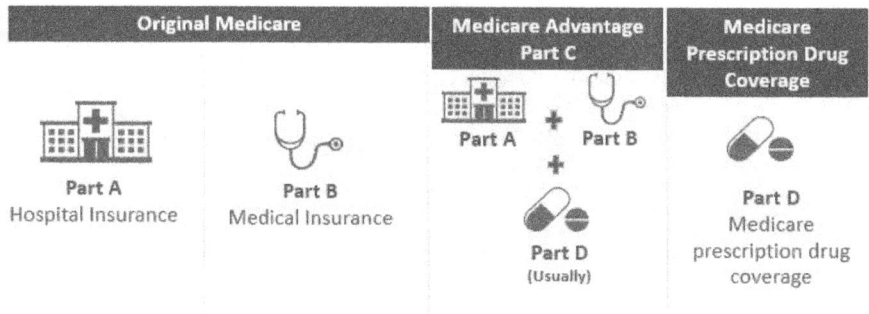

Original Medicare		Medicare Advantage Part C	Medicare Prescription Drug Coverage

Part A
Hospital Insurance

Part B
Medical Insurance

Part A + Part B
+
Part D
(Usually)

Part D
Medicare prescription drug coverage

"The Four Parts of Medicare" retrieved from: *Medicare and You 2023*

Chart #2

A quick look at your Medicare coverage choices

There are 2 main choices for how you get your Medicare coverage. These choices will be explained in more detail on the next page and throughout this book.

Option 1: Original Medicare	Option 2: Medicare Advantage (Part C)
(See pages 61–64) This includes Part A and B.	*(See pages 65–78)* These plans are like HMOs or PPOs, and typically include Part A, B, and D.

Option 1: Original Medicare

Part A
Hospital Insurance

+

Part B
Medical Insurance

You can add:
(See pages 83–96)

Part D
Medicare Prescription Drug Coverage

You can also add:
(See pages 79–82)

Medigap
Medicare Supplement Insurance
(Medigap policies help pay your out-of-pocket costs in Original Medicare.)

Option 2: Medicare Advantage (Part C)

Part A
Hospital Insurance

+

Part B
Medical Insurance

+

Part D
Medicare Prescription Drug Coverage

(Most plans cover prescription drugs. If yours doesn't, you may be able to join a separate Part D plan.)

"Two Pathways of Medicare" retrieved from: *Medicare and You 2023*

Chart #3

Medicare Supplement Insurance (Medigap) Plans										
Benefits	A	B	C	D	F*	G	K	L	M	N
Part A coinsurance and hospital costs (up to an additional 365 days after Medicare benefits are used up)	100%	100%	100%	100%	100%	100%	100%	100%	100%	100%
Part B coinsurance or copayment	100%	100%	100%	100%	100%	100%	50%	75%	100%	100%***
Blood (first 3 pints)	100%	100%	100%	100%	100%	100%	50%	75%	100%	100%
Part A hospice care coinsurance or copayment	100%	100%	100%	100%	100%	100%	50%	75%	100%	100%
Skilled nursing facility care coinsurance			100%	100%	100%	100%	50%	75%	100%	100%
Part A deductible		100%	100%	100%	100%	100%	50%	75%	50%	100%
Part B deductible			100%		100%					
Part B excess charges					100%	100%				
Foreign travel emergency (up to plan limits)			80%	80%	80%	80%			80%	80%
Out-of-Pocket Limit in 2023**							$6,940	$3,470		

"Medicare Supplement Insurance" retrieved from: *Medicare and You 2023*

Chart #4

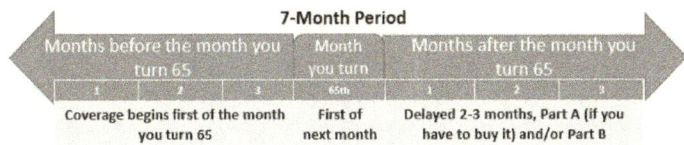

7-Month Period

Months before the month you turn 65			Month you turn	Months after the month you turn 65		
1	2	3	65th	1	2	3

Coverage begins first of the month you turn 65 — First of next month — Delayed 2-3 months, Part A (if you have to buy it) and/or Part B

"When to Enroll in Medicare" retrieved from: *Medicare and You 2023*

Chart # 5

**"Part B Premiums" retrieved from: *Medicare and You 2023*
"Part B Premiums for Joint and Separate Returns"
retrieved from: *Medicare Premiums***

If your yearly income in 2021 (for what you pay in 2023) was:			You pay each month (in 2022)
File individual tax return	File joint tax return	File married & separate tax return	
$97,000 or less	$194,000 or less	$97,000 or less	$164.90
above $97,000 up to $123,000	above $194,000 up to $246,000	Not applicable	$230.80
above $123,000 up to $153,000	above $246,000 up to $306,000	Not applicable	$329.70
above $153,000 up to $183,000	above $306,000 up to $366,000	Not applicable	$428.60
above $183,000 up to $500,000	above $366,000 up to $750,000	above $91,000 and less than $409,000	$527.50
above $500,000	above $750,000	$409,000 and above	$560.50

**Get more information about your Part B premium from
Social Security [PDF, 341 KB].**

Chart # 6

"Part D Premiums" retrieved from: *Medicare and you 2023* "Part D Premiums for Join and Separate Returns" retrieved from: *Medicare Premiums*

If your filing status and yearly income in 2021 was			
File individual tax return	File joint tax return	File married & separate tax return	You pay each month (in 2022)
$97,000 or less	$194,000 or less	$97,000 or less	your plan premium
above $97,000 up to $123,000	above $194,000 up to $246,000	not applicable	$12.20 + your plan premium
above $123,000 up to $153,000	above $246,000 up to $306,000	not applicable	$31.50 + your plan premium
above $153,000 up to $170,000	above $306,000 up to $366,000	not applicable	$50.70 + your plan premium
above $183,000 and less than $500,000	above $366,000 and less than $750,000	above $97,000 and less than $409,000	$70.00 + your plan premium
$500,000 or above	$750,000 and above	$409,000 and above	$76.40 + your plan premium

Chart # 7

If you have **retiree** insurance (insurance from your or your spouse's former employment) ...	Medicare pays first.
If you are age 65 or older, have group health plan coverage based on your or your spouse's **current** employment, and the employer has **20 or more employees**...	Your group health plan pays first.
If you are age 65 or older, have group health plan coverage based on your or your spouse's **current** employment, and the employer has **less than 20 employees**...	Medicare pays first.
If you are under age 65 and disabled, have group health plan coverage based on your, a spouse's, or a family member's **current** employment, and the employer has **100 or more employees**...	Your group health plan pays first.
If you are under age 65 and disabled, have group health plan coverage based on your or a family member's **current** employment, and the employer has **less than 100 employees**...	Medicare pays first.
If you have Medicare because of End-Stage Renal Disease (ESRD)...	Your group health plan will pay first for the first 30 months after you become eligible to enroll in Medicare. Medicare will pay first after this 30-month period.

Chart # 8

15 SNP-Specific Chronic Conditions:

1. Chronic alcohol and other drug dependence

2. Autoimmune disorders limited to:

   o Polyarteritis nodosa

   o Polymyalgia rheumatica

   o Polymyositis

   o Rheumatoid arthritis

   o Systemic lupus erythematosus

3. Cancer, excluding pre-cancer conditions or in-situ status

4. Cardiovascular disorders limited to:

   o Cardiac arrhythmias

   o Coronary artery disease

   o Peripheral vascular disease

   o Chronic venous thromboembolic disorder

5. Chronic heart failure

6. Dementia

7. Diabetes mellitus

8. End-stage liver disease

9. End-stage renal disease (ESRD) requiring dialysis

10. Severe hematologic disorders limited to:

    o Aplastic anemia

    o Hemophilia

    o Immune thrombocytopenic purpura

    o Myelodysplastic syndrome

    o Sickle-cell disease (excluding sickle-cell trait)

11. HIV/AIDS

12. Chronic lung disorders limited to

    o Asthma

    o Chronic bronchitis

    o Emphysema

    o Pulmonary fibrosis

    o Pulmonary hypertension

13. Chronic and disabling mental health conditions limited to:

    o Bipolar disorders

    o Major depressive disorders

    o Paranoid disorder

    o Schizophrenia

    o Schizoaffective disorder

14. Neurologic disorders limited to

    o Amyotrophic lateral sclerosis (ALS)

    o Epilepsy

    o Extensive paralysis (i.e., hemiplegia, quadriplegia, paraplegia, monoplegia)

    o Huntington's disease

    o Multiple sclerosis

    o Parkinson's disease

    o Polyneuropathy

    o Spinal stenosis

    o Stroke-related neurologic deficit

15. Stroke

Where can I go for more information?

Broome, H. (2018). *Get it r.i.g.h.t. blog: Mondays with Mr. Medicare*. Retrieved from:
www.mcknightadvisory.com/get-it-right

Centers for Medicare and Medicaid Services. (2017, November). *Medicare and You 2021*. Retrieved from: https://www.medicare.gov/pubs/pdf/10050-Medicare-and-You.pdf

Centers for Medicare and Medicaid Services. (2017, September). *Medicare & other health benefits: Your guide to who pays first*. Retrieved from:
https://www.medicare.gov/Pubs/pdf/02179-Medicare-Coordination-Benefits-Payer.pdf

Centers for Medicare and Medicaid Services. (2018, June). *2018 choosing a medigap policy: A guide to health insurance for people with Medicare*. Retrieved from:
https://www.medicare.gov/Pubs/pdf/02110-Medicare-Medigap.guide.pdf

Centers for Medicare and Medicaid Services. (2013, May). *2013 national training program: Module 1 understanding Medicare*. Retrieved from:
https://www.cms.gov/Outreach-and-Education/Training/CMSNationalTrainingProgram/Downloads/2013-Understanding-Medicare-Workbook.pdf

Centers for Medicare and Medicaid Services. (2018). *Cms.gov: Centers for Medicare & Medicaid services*. Retrieved from: https://www.cms.gov

Social Security Administration. (2018). *Social Security*. Retrieved from:
https://www.ssa.gov/

Social Security Administration. (2018, January). *Medicare premiums: Rules for higher-income beneficiaries.* Retrieved from: https://www.ssa.gov/pubs/EN-05-10536.pdf

Social Security Administration. (2017, December). *Form ssa-44: Medicare income-related monthly adjustment amount – life-changing event form.* Retrieved from:
https://www.ssa.gov/forms/ssa-44.pdf

U.S. Centers for Medicare and Medicaid Services. (2018). *Medicare.gov: The official U.S. government site for Medicare.* Retrieved from:
https://www.medicare.gov

U.S. Department of Health and Human Services. (2018, January). *Your Medicare benefits.* Retrieved from:
https://www.medicare.gov/Pubs/pdf/10116-Your-Medicare-Benefits.pdf